Place in Space

Dana DeFranco

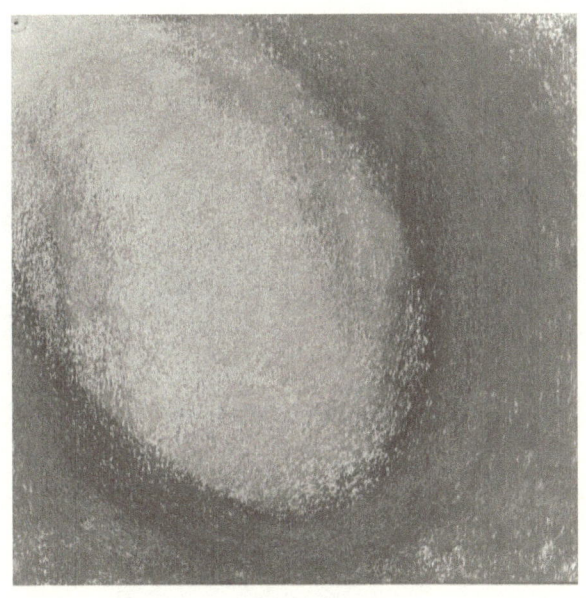

SPUYTEN DUYVIL

New York City

Library of Congress Control Number: 2025931518

for: us

Space

Open Seating: Outtakes

a mathematician[1] and an anarchist[2]

      walk into a bar

they grab seats close enough
      so that their knees won't hit

who will liberate us
      from our liberators

a conscience. in spirit. in step. in solidarity
      when we take in
            our own hands
            our own good
               and happiness.

let's. let us. stare into pages
      these gestures: *the vanquished do not die*

      because this is not bound
      because pages look   back
      because poems can never be bound and
          pages stare back   eventually

you think we are incomplete
      in all our complex forms. you believe we are
      incomplete

---

1 Nicanor Parra from *Antipoems/Jokes to Mislead the Police*
2 Virgilia D'Andrea from *The Vanquished Who Do Not Die/Tormento*

still, the dirt smells so fresh and clean

  perfectly flawed

    perfectly flawed is the perfection

because I am here
because I exist
  because I have roots

some argue whether we exist in time
    whether or not we hold the divine
      in the lining of our chests

what I know is that perfection is perfectly flawed
while it's the beast in a big fat car that has the keys
and everything continues to smell bad
  what's the worst is for a lifetime:

    traversing shops / markets
      looking at the windows
& the dirt smells so clean and fresh
      floating along this earth

what are these feathers that make us want to fly
  what happens when we leave our hearts behind

all the food to feed
  all the food to share

  a roll with butter for dessert
  a floor with a large heater

a place to belong and
            driven mad

                        mad is a mad woman
          beautifully perfected and flawed

Motherless mothers raise mothers   motherless
      when we are all mothers / we are mothers
                              tumors grow along the inside
                              tubes that eat at time

                        taking time

              this is the time it takes

            perfectly flawed is the perfection

      I am here
      I exist
      I have

      roots in the air. now. floating along this earth

      and the dirt smells so fresh and clean

      as I float along the earth

Tuck

Tuck |tək| verb often used with prepositions *in* or *away* **1 to** be aware of loosened membranes along measured lines: *She tucked her feelings inside her thighs* **2** to stitch up your genitals (& ass cheeks) to avoid detection: *He finally gave in to tucking it all in* **3** to activate a safety precaution against unwanted hands: *Tucking in your lungs becomes easier with time*

*Note: Tucking comes in many shades;
                        available in indigo upon request

And so it is

      just like that,

a fledgling
lifts its eyes

because I looked up
because it was there, trapped in the dusty window
      that is not quite a window
because its strings pull up and down
because *they* remind me that these are the same
      strings on the houses on spring street

and the only thing that holds everything together are   these stories

because I never lived there

      and still sing the story of strings

strings find ways to   travel the distance

strings *don't like* to be cut

strings *do not belong* being cut
            you can   never cut strings

strings keep the *feeling of belonging*

the string belongs to the strummer of the stringer

the stringer holds the strings

            the strings are strung by strummer

the strummer strums the strings

dear bird:

i looked up and found your eyes

you were caught / trapped / or maybe

just there

i want you to imagine me for a moment

what I need is for this to make sense

that I impart something here

Dreaming

I landed on   a photo.
It was an article that told me about
        how to live.

I crossed into the lines & folded myself outside the dots

And then I turned into a bird

> *the bird was unfortunately pregnant—*
> *she turned out to be a girl*
> *the indivisible genitals—*

saddened, her dark breast
pushed longingly
against the fever of the moon.

I stepped outside its feathers,
     I bled outside its wings
          the spell of disbelief,
               tucked and sold to
       whatever touched   me back

for a time   against my own

divination

     to leave and fly   and come back

to fly away   and come back

to fly

               and come away

and back again   to fly

Then came the sound.

The most horrible sound
      as if the bird had never spoken before:

            awkward bird
            with songs of doubt
            with sounds rebounding

                of doubt songs

the feathers
      on the ground
      proved its
          flight

              little bird,

     now pulling seeds

       from a flower stalk /

I broke the silence of
the eyes

        for what they thought

        the bird *possessed*

        was nothing

and it was nothing

       this thing,

       a belly with a creation &

          no one knew how it

             even got there

I explained how seeds get planted
           by the wind.

           I explained that things grow here

                                        & there and

                                        just end up
                                        in places

because the wind doesn't have hands
the wind has no intentions   I explained

with that, the bird sat down
        with an impound of
               sounds:

they come to us and drown us. they drown us so we fight. we fight for flight. but the fight tires us. numbs us. makes us scared of everything.

they feed us. give us water when we want food. food when we have thirst. they blast water and grow us what we need. with hands. their hands. our hands. empty hands. hateful hands. jealous hands. hands that trick and deprive. hands that want to take it all away. we learn to fold ourselves outside the dots. we fold ourselves outside the lines / these lines are not real lines

we carry the space on our backs
we fly between the dots /
we slip through the broken lines /

                              because these are not lines

we fly between the notes and drown out the sounds
we wash the echoes in aquifers
          and shades of indigo

we learn that
wherever there is love
          it's from the other side

we don't even know our real names and   still

we are always here   together

          just breathing

I faced the bird and gestured
   with loud complex hands

                  for the bird to live and love

     it stood sadly for a moment

      then smiled

            until it pooped

  and flew away.

FUCK

Fuck, |fək| noun (countable) **see fuckery**
1 an emphatic gesture sometimes called reactive:
Look at these fucks 2 the intergenerational
satisfaction of passionate appeal: *What the fuck
did you just say?* 3 the conjuring of newfound
episodes that strum the heart into maintaining
beat: *She says she doesn't give a fuck, but I
know she still cares* 4 penetrating occasions
characterized by madness: *The fuckery never ends*
5 sensory overload due to a commitment to seeing
all things to the end: *This is the last time you'll see
me give a fuck*

Fuck |fək| verb (transitive & intransitive)
participles fucking, fucked 1 to push someone
or something out of the realm of comfort: *They
are just fucking with you* 2 to ingest what many
consider unsavory or unwanted: *That really
fucked me up, but I'm so much better now that
you're here* 3 to convolute or reproach (in an altered
state of consciousness) what would otherwise be
tolerated: *You could fuck up a free lunch*

Relax & enjoy it

Eyes upon eyes upon eyes upon eyes *(lively tempo)*

Eyes upon eyes
Eyes upon eyes

Eyes upon eyes upon eyes upon eyes

Eyes upon eyes *(playful)*
Eyes upon eyes

Eyes upon eyes upon eyes upon eyes *(slow the tempo)*
Eyes upon eyes /eyes upon eyes

Eyes upon / eyes upon /eyes upon /eyes *(freestyle)*

Eyes / upon *(crawling whisper)*
eyes /
upon / eyes /
upon / eyes

(Refrain)

Out and About

Note to self: Never forget your sketchpad. It keeps your hands busy. Makes you look like less of a loner. Or you could just order a stiff drink. And, if you had your sketchpad, you wouldn't be tempted to say these things out loud:

How would you like it if I shove my walker up your ass?

What is the telekinetic meaning of your black beret when you're wearing Sketchers?

Why do I always feel better when someone who looks like me acknowledges this with the unspoken way of knowing that they are thinking the same thing?

How do I feel comfortable in this seat?

How do I not feel isolated?

What the fuck are you staring at?

I really miss my dad.

Word: Mother

what is a mother?

       how much of my tit do you want to suck off of?

apparently,
       I have sucked
              too much, too little,
              and *sometimes* not enough—

my tongue is guilty and shamed and
sometimes

I'm told   *sometimes* that I'm
       a joy,
            and I'm reminded
            that my mother
            is the craziest bitch I know.

every day I listen to how *the world is*
fucked up / inside out. it's eat or
be eaten / gotta learn to survive, dolly

whatcha gonna do, dane?
whatcha gonna eat?
I sent you cans of sardines
Dad loved sardines
yea, I miss Dad, too
yea, dolly. But not like me

so what is a mother? a person
you can go out
        to drinks with
                in the summer.
one night. she asked the bartender
to recommend
        a good red.
we sat at the bar. it was dark.
we drank. Got the bill from
Bill.
        50 dollars for two glasses of wine.
        my mom loses her shit. I call her Buzzy.
she asks the bartender
        what the fuck is wrong with you!
        how do you sell someone a 20-dollar glass of wine without asking?
the receipt turns into a snowstorm
        flurries all over the bar
the security comes
eyes everywhere

so what is a mother?
a woman who starts trouble wherever she goes
        because she doesn't know how to behave.

But I do.

And so she lives,
        and I'm stranded:
stranded here
        stranded there &

        I really do love my mother

Comfort and Joy
(Leaves and parting words)

The world is a piece of shit
        and so is Facebook

"Oh, happy birthday, Sarah"
"I just ate a sandwich"
"Look! We just went to the zoo"

       who gives a fuck

And then I gotta look at --------
        in that coat?
Some fox or poor other animal &
        I was going to ask her
what the fuck corpse her
        husband hung around
          her shoulders
            but I let it go

I look at the devastation that this botox-filled
        piece of dreck
has done to destroy / I ask
        how does this happen? but this is
nothing new

       the barbarians are running the world

In my next life, I want to understand all this
and if I read all these books,
        I would be a fucking genius.

I buy books I would like to read
and look at them on the shelf and say:
I could have READ that.

Your father bought me one book.
It's called *Simple Abundance: A Daybook of Comfort and Joy*
He brought it to me one day so that
I could turn over a
new leaf

if I read anything, it will be this

Do you ever walk around
thinking you need a   *blood transfusion*

when really
you just need to

throw your

shoes
away

and start

fresh

Witness

It's on the same day I saw a
Porsche run into a pedestrian,
left lying there on his side

people went
to sit by him
while others pulled away,
            not the blankets, *but*
the comfort offered by strangers,
            how strange
was the estrangement
            as we, as I watched
from the bus, screaming and calling 911

Porsche driver, not approaching
the person hurt there,
            the person he actually killed
after tailing a car, the car that
            finally slammed on its brakes in the rain,
everywhere wet and uneasy from
            pushing up so hard
aggressive in the expensive,
            hateful car that
hydroplaned onto
            the curb populated
and riddled with people—
            you were driving so fast
through the intersection /

I remember your shorts
and tennis shoes
through the slippery rain,
  your arrogance, &
    you weren't even crying.

All day long, I reminded myself
that this could have been me—
  hit someone with my car,
hurt someone
  not meaning to

and then back on the bus,
  a different line at the end of
the day and today,
that day, with lots of
chatter from a mechanic
  talking to all the passengers
warning us that
  even though *the freeway*
is the most hazardous place on earth,
  the thing that causes
the greatest loss, the loss he
  calls death,

  is speed

that the most dangerous thing is
  to change a tire on *the freeway*
having trained hundreds
  how to do this in his lifetime
   and here to talk about it

I saw how proud he was
          to be a teacher,
but maybe he was more proud
          to be alive
knowing that skillfulness
          isn't everywhere
and ignored
          just the same

I feel the months of death mounting
between gunshots and machinery
          cars and guns,
          between
Buffalo and Uvalde
          all of these people
          all of these children

we are told that officers *made the wrong call*
          also known as the wrong decision

and I recall what the mechanic said about speed
knowing how it kills,
thinking how quickly speed can save
          just as easily as it does otherwise
knowing how many guns
          lived in a place
                    that stood by and
                              held silent

Late to work

I got off at
Civic Center,
Bart, the usual
and raining
           ground was slippery
                     and then
I heard the scream /
           the sound. Familiar sound.
The bug sound.
And I try to ignore it because
           I can't be late for work.

I'm walking so fast past the SFPL,
passing whatever the buildings, and almost
at the trees and it's the unrelenting sensation

so I go back / went back and
met the sound / beautiful fully grown worm,
stranded on the pavement

        my poor baby

so I took you
and put you in the grass and
all felt right in the world
—late to work
my supervisor asked me why
and all she said was ok
with a beautiful look
in her dark brown eyes.

I said thank you, walking casually
into the bathroom

because it's   just not

        easy this way

Oh, not so fast

This little fucker has all the women fawning over him with his adorable face and bright blond hair, the bluest of eyes and a marvel mask.

He is scrubbed clean and his hair is parted perfectly on the side with maybe some kind of gel.

He is getting professional haircuts.

No one is taking a buzzer to his shit.

No one is complaining about how much he costs.

The cost of him

          How he's driving them to the poor house

          Just for needing a haircut and some shoes and a

sweater

And he is well taken care of by his nanny—a passenger asks: asks his name and he answers without skipping a beat

Will he remember who raised him
        her fat hands

her fat hands
        her nails aren't done
        her shoes are dirty, but
she stays still

will he

remember who raised him? who he is on the
      inside?

          what will he stand for/

            stand up to

                stand behind

            stand up to

                stand with

            stand in sight of

who will he be

      who will he   love

and what   will he touch with his

    own grown hands

will he have macho hair

will he value the

power of hands

     over

         the power of big lots

whose wheels

go round

   and round

Coming & Going (in parts)

COMING (7:58 AM)

You and your fucking dog park
   and I love dogs   but you and you &
   you &   *your fucking dog park*

 and I really love animals   but I can't take you
 and you and you & you   and *your fucking dog*
   park

what if your dog turned around and
   ate your face
     or turned around and
      stood up

What if the dog became a two-legged and put *you*
   on all fours?

   So, maybe walking would be hard at first, but
   how would you handle this

    if you were to handle this at all?

Would you scream and ask for forgiveness
   or would you
     take your place
      & return the favor

would you beg to be scratched
     & rubbed
          doing anything for a treat
        or would you

smell every ass of each passerby hoping for
        just the right cocktail to
       send you

          swooning

GOING (4:58 PM)

If it's all organic   then why does everything
                                feel so—

this thing we do   the things we do
                                like

when you help someone because you are cornered into helping
someone that you don't even know when you are trapped and liter-
ally suffocating and you know it's the right thing to do even though
you are so uncomfortable and incredibly sad. And you tap this per-
son's shoulder because the very old woman asks you to

      not with her words
           but with her eyes and gestures
because the big guy won't answer her hand gestures
because the big guy won't answer since it's not English

So, you join the party on the dance floor and throw your hands in
the air and reach over with your right arm extended just so and ever
so gently as you go ahead and put a finger in the very corner of the
man's dirty jacket where the stitching seems to be extra thick so he
might not feel you and this whole situation could disappear and
then you hear
Yeah. I'll move and don't ever touch me again
        because he knew all along that everyone was waiting for
him to move
        because he was reveling in the power of his silence, feigning

the invisibility of her language to ridicule the sick old man who just
needed to sit down   because his body was so big and tall his
jacket the color of war and to deal with his brush of hate you burst
out a pathetic explanation as if wanting to be forgiven

    because I only tapped your shoulder
    because you were ignoring her

        even though you knew she was trying to get
        your attention

    because at some point
    she became really furious.

She and (we) & I became so furious that he wasn't responding so
she tapped my shoulder to tell me to tell him to get up and move
so her sick husband could sit down in the section reserved for the
elderly and she wouldn't let me give him my seat even though I tried
    because she rendered me *disabled*
& with that I couldn't stop that thing that had been forming in my
eye so I just sat silent as I looked up at the ceiling and let it roll
down to the floor.

Of this, becomes will

when things go wrong.
things go right.
        intermezzo—they cheer.
bring in the drunks. the banished. the ones that really under-
stand. bring in the newbies. the vets.

      Vast are the bastards that wait at the gate.
      Vast are the vultures that watch while we wait.
      Vast are the features with their ugly, dry skin.
      Vast are the hopeless, who cry deep within.

PLACE

Place |plās| noun **1** where *the act of being tucked*
is registered and accumulates like yeast: *What is
it like to live and work in this place?* **2** a designation
passed off as *inherent, hereditary or otherwise
specified* especially when ambiguity exists: *You
look like you (filler) belong in this place* **3** any
telekinetic adjustment to matter often enacting
dissociative states; omniscient narrator in the third
person required: *This is a place of business, so
check your emotions at the door* **4** an analysis of
complexion plus the size of one's thighs to assess
potential: *"Your place or mine"* **5** the phenomenology
of worth: *This must be the place*

Place |plās| verb **1** to hide or situate a thought,
feeling or intention: *Place it in plain view so no
one will see it* **2** to dislocate space: *The freeway
will be placed here* **3** to impose parameters that
often, *but not always*, draw crowds of onlookers:
They plan to place self-driving cars downtown
4 to commodify and yearn for more: *We are placing
teacher housing on the old navy base*

*Note: Place needs space; space does not need place

Time's Tabled

there was a time when all I cared about was pleasure. feeling good.
making you feel good.

caring about how you were feeling   *more than my own*

and now
        there is nothing left to feel

and I see photos of you holding things
        things that you hold
                now glazed
                        in clean dirt

these are the things I hold on to
these are the things I used to hold
these are the things I can no longer hold or carry

        because I dropped them & I can't retrace my steps

just to say that
        I no longer count the phases of the moon

that now,
        I can't even see my own feet

Let's Make a Deal

Disclaimer:
sales are for salvation purposes only,
surveillance not included

handmade
homemade
local & artisanal
consciously   created,

      4 time *management*
           acquisitions &
                assemblies

come one, come all, we're
free of charge, just spin
the wheel:
      land a place that taunts /
           a place that needs /
                a place that places /

pound a hand and demand
      divisions &
           crises for the table

hands (preposition) the table
      hands all around

           this

place

Logic

I know you,
you know me
come quick into my
house.

You know me,
I know you
show me to your
house.

I am me,
you are you
sleep deep inside my
house.

You are you,
I am me
we slink around your
house.

You are me
& i am you
it's time to think our
house.

i am you,
but you're not me
we separate our
house.

Sign up, sign below—
sign this

        for me.
    I think they don't
want me to raise my hand,
    anymore,

    well, it's not like
they ever called on me

anyway

On Chestnut:
what if Ziggy Stardust, Live in the Marina, SF

it looks like people have changed their pants for good
accessible wants and wares for the good of   the lockdown

insta-things,
            some things
                        to. be. locked. down. for. good.

pants, once called leggings or
            yoga pants   *as some say*

            are now called simply: pants

some call these party pants or hot pants
even though they are for   work   pants
and work pants can't be hot or
                        can they?

these pants are
            smiling lightening
                        insta-pants good for home or office
in the home office / working from home and
                                    some home for good
so, say goodbye to your pants suit:
                        no longer suited for walks around the dog park

big bad dog by your side as you
            slide and glide past potholes
                        and loopy sidewalks / pants with

the *mass appeal*

day after day   the morning brew
where dogs gather for their meet and greet because
                    they actually know each other fully

            cross-fit along the *smell of*
                    what *used to be a coffee shop*
collars full of bling & better love because

this is the love that sparkles: not in their eyes,
            but chains around their necks.

A friend told me there is a new surgery available

        surgery with a perma-feel   because

        Houston, we have a problem:

        Vaginas to mission control

        Oh, the camel toe will never do!

& into the force of life we go
        blasting past beautiful little nests
            clean breaks
                to the origins of time

                and this time, it's time to scale back the skin,

                    the bulky chunky outer folds

this time: **the labia majora**

the skin is   bulging

the skin is   popping   out

making this insta-pant fashion thing a dance of the pants and

very much a challenge
        because what's getting stuck
        in the middle of this
        frontal wedgie is a *space oddity*
                and nonetheless important

because someone out there might feel like having kids

        At some point women
                set the world   ablaze & now,
                this is insta-life
                        with doubty pouty lippy looks
                        & don't mess with the Marina chicks

        with their sound buttocks built stronger
                with squats and maybe yoga /
        weights & resistance to weight
                & weight resistance
        these flabby little pieces
                can't be liquidated with B-12 or laser
& since you can't lose weight from your **labia majora**,
        the surgery is a sure solution,

but what we still don't know is whether
      a penis can fit into these
            legging yoga pant things
                        because

I think that would look smashing

maybe this is what we already call ballet

           or *dancing in the dark*:

     no, not like Springsteen
        and his worker-body jeans

but more like Bowie
        because

     you've got your mother in a whirl /
       she's not sure if you're a boy or a girl

so put them on you tacky thing   & bulge that junk

       keep it all high and   high flying
                  fly high
                     & ever so real,

             you lovely,

        tacky

      things

Committed to Public Education
(The Coat Closet: Tote bags
and other forms of recognition)

As a way of showing
our deepest
gratitude,
as a way of giving
our deepest of
thanks,
to you /
and you /
and yes, you over there
licking crumbs off that
        Styrofoam plate

with this mic
we invite you
to get up & grab
            a tote bag &
fill it with pencils
and (smirk) yes,
stolen napkins &
whatever leftovers—

Remember: the world is yours

because we know that
you are in a battle of sorts
that you move
        in a long list of targets
                that conjure in the smalls of your

backs,
so we thank you
    with a bag
        that you can carry

because such is the nature of bags

and empty hands

Plastic Couches
(Candy jars: strings tied to things
that go nowhere)

Women
        marriage

bad relationships
        no love lost

women marriage
        anyway

these commercials
        anyway

money
        commercials
what's the
        the latest word for

                WTF,

I am sick of the word amazing

We are tired
We are tired

Let's put on the ceiling fan

        and cool ourselves

                into breezy collision

Let's nest
(Yards: hair threads)

I deliberately throw my hair into
            the dirt, hoping that
                  one day,

it will end up in a bird's nest.

I picture a family living there—
            that is, in the strands of
                  my hair.

A family good at all the
            family stuff,

no competition
to electrify nights
            at Christmas /

these aren't
            yes birds /

I wonder
            if they kiss their children

or poop on
            other birds

do they sing to each other

            or demand time for privacy

do they walk each other out
      on a hot
            summer's night /

I hope
      they like my hair

that it meets their expectations

that I make the grade
      for nests woven for
whatever the bird reason /

pulling hard from the back of my hair
      the curliest and darkest parts

that they might find these
      pieces most appealing

not knowing how they choose
which threads they want
      to build with

or how they distinguish
quality materials
      within the void

of junk

Platforms

There are those who
        leave
and those who
        stay

There are people who
want to
        leave
but stay

We stay
        even when
we want to
        leave

We want to leave
        and we
stay   still

There are those
        who say

they didn't
want to
        leave

they leave /
        say they
wanted to
        stay

they leave /
saying they wanted
    to stay

          put
in the distance
    between what
a fork or spoon
    allows
between a hand
    and a mouth
it's the range measured
    in the distance
between hands
    and mouths

the long and narrow
    journey from
your hand to my mouth

each time we stay
    and you
        leave

Pound for Pound

There is a song by the modern lovers
      and it goes something like
             da da da— some people try to pick up girls
             & they get called an asshole /
             dah dah dah &
                    Pablo Picasso was never called an asshole

The question begs:

was Pablo Picasso never called an asshole?
…..

      which brings me back to other assholes such as
Ted Kaczynski

was Ted Kaczynski ever called an asshole?
Oh, for sure!

What is the logic here?
Well, for one Ted comes from a Catholic family
    who later became atheists,   *this could have done it*

Or what about the fact that his father was a
sausage maker

I want to know what he was so angry   about

and was he even angry is *my* question
       what upset him and
              what was he upset   about

because Ted taught at UC Berkeley
was excellent in math and the sciences:
       he did seek revenge   though

Did he not understand that the world isn't just for him? That other people need to live here too? That he was so entangled in his own fucking weirdness that he couldn't see that we— any of us— could blow up and die from one of his stupid little tricks?

I think about this: let's consider
why one person cares and another doesn't
       why one person is a hero, the other a villain
             why one is an asshole and the other not
What are we gauging as standards when
       Janet Reno's mom wrestled alligators— fun fact!
          and look at the success she became.
The truth is that there is nothing 'crazy' about Ted. Actually, he
is quite common. *the common man. the common man. the common*
man that can.

When we gauge what is swinging or tucked in *down there* maybe
we lean into the chemicals that surge and flow all around &
through us. that these chemicals cause reactions. that these
chemicals are blamed when we run out of answers.

some call us animals / that we brutalize each other because we are
animals: someone reminded me that cute little ducks rape other
little ducks. male ducks. rape. females. female. ducks. I wonder

why they even valued this enough to repeat it
> that the standards set by ducks would have anything to do
> *with us*

because like ducks, we brutalize each other. maybe
it's because we don't know God / or we weren't loved enough or
even properly. some say they had to leave a mark on this lonely
place. some say the earth wanted things done to it. and then there
are some who prefer to get a bag of chips and go straight for the
couch. turn on the tv. disappear. completely.

& there are those who don't want to disappear. & no matter how
hard we try, people come and people go. some of us will cry for
those now gone. because we won't be able to 'move on' because
there is no moving on. because there is no place to go. there is no
other place. we can carve this world up into a million pieces. we
can abuse hate and abandon each other. and still: we are here. &
I don't want to die. I'm going to live and breathe. make mistakes.
get up the next day. look at myself in the mirror. regret the things
I said. go over the same shit over & over in my head. and then get
a phone call. and it's from someone I love. and this strange feeling
that no one can quite explain is what keeps me moving.

The facts are as the facts remain:
Ted was a bigot   a racist   a homophobe

& Pablo was *a womanizer,*
> abusing and using, abusing to use

> but Pablo wasn't
> blowing up
> > rich man's hands
> > > with mail:

& this is why

Pablo Picasso

was never called

an asshole

Vocalizing

The cadence of your voice
I hear you and
      I get it.

I look and see how you are in the winner's seat

I make you uncomfortable in my silence

                            it's an energy thing.

When you are born on the right or wrong side.
On the right side of the wrong and the wrong   right.

This isn't left.

The right written side of the wrong shouldn't be
      what's left.

The good.
The bad.

The kiddy pool that you pee in.
      You pee in telepathic waves.
         Like a cat.

No one wants to know your inner workings. They have a place for you.

So we stick wood in
      upright
and build toilets and all of it is
      property

when it is actually
just land

and I like your land—and

no one really likes you anyway
but pipes
remain
for shits and
bitters,
for lovers
beholden to
their scars

SPACE

Space |spās| noun **1** that which is broken by
place: *This space is reserved for VIP only*
2 the taste and smell of velvet: *This is the
space* **3** an area or field of non-place; the
potential for authenticity: *I see better in that
space vs. this space* **4** any bubble-forming
substance, especially air available in underwater
dispensers: *It's not you, it's me. I just need some
space*

Space |spās| verb: **1** to position things in place in
order to disrupt space: *They don't understand
that they must space the vegetables with flowers*
2 to visualize ventures fueled by bloodthirst,
disguised as wanderlust: *It is said things are spaced
like /this & that/ to create opportunities to live and
even thrive*

*Note: Space does not need place

Transmission

Doors live in walled space
       doors hold a place
we travel through spaces
       that are walled
we walk through walls in spaces
       sometimes called doors

Places place us in the space of
      passageways &
      pathways
      pathfinders &
         finders' fees
            fees waived &
         waived fees
            fee-for-service
               services rendered
                rendered targets
                 target practice
              practice makes perfect
             practice makes permanent
               permanent markers
                marking time
                time out
                    for
                time
                 travel

Woken rubble, songs lost by lovebirds ingested in flight

Space

suit. Space

monkey. Spaced out.

Out of place. Place

mats. Material girl. Gin and

syrup. Symbolic mergers. Mercurial antibodies. Antlers

and chilblains. Chilled bread. Breaking habits. Habeas corpus. Corridors and empty chairs. Charlatans and peacocks. Peals and seals. Seamless treasures. Trenchant undulation. Untitled scales screaming stop / stoned cans calling your name in full preparation.

The Death of Ground Control

sandstorms wink and (*one*)
we came prepared (*counting up*)
leave the capsule (*two*)
step out into the sea (*three*)
walk along and don't look back

fish scales and wings (*four*)
our spacecraft knows the way (*five*)
engines are on (*six*)
an arm to the sky (*seven*)
feathers, shields and microwaves

space embryo (*eight*)
fibrous go-go goddess (*nine*)
click ignition (*ten*)
outer edges don't hold (*go*)
ash to bone and lives erased

future arrows and
love you thought was gone (*liftoff*)
finally has a chance
lifting up into the air
counting forward so we can
    drift into the past.

For the love of

bugs / and so
I was walking in for my third shot,
& I heard this familiar cry—
            familiar
it's like a silent ringing,
this cry I know / the cry that rounds—
think of moth mouths and earthworms
the sound of sound

maybe in this poem you understand
that I hear
the pain of insects

I hear their love songs
too

and so on this day
with my walker to
balance myself /
I heard the familiar cry—
the onlookers
the walker & the cry I can't explain.

Looking down
        pink ball,
                peppercorn
the scream,
        leaning down, I
balance myself and my ugly dress
all made of shitty fabrics

I bent down and a ladybug
climbed onto my hand /
& I was
          wondering where we were going /
saying yes to where we went

& I placed us in the grass

A Bassline, Refreshed

Clash the find(er)'s fee
      finding whatever

      can be found

and fin(er)
      than before

take the skin off the beast

      mine is what I find

      all fine /

better left
      & buried

      hidden in the weeds

come join
      the lonesome world

where loving you is pleasure
where loving us
         is free

Hope

Caterpillar eyes,
     surrender your hands
     and broken wristbands

     so that your feet
     lay rest like
     handlebars—

     watch me
     upside down

     in this darkness

be sad no more

bubbles speak
     this forest green,

shapes of silk and wings of candy—

be sad no more

join the moonlight,
     your bridge against my cheek,

the look of disgust and purple sorrows -

elapse this moment

as if it were

a mountain,
swallows slipping free
along the howls of your hair

elapse

and be
no more

Make it last

Don't hand me your   dog tags,
instead
        hand me   you

I heard that love poem 1013 reads:

        I can take your pain away

Nudity Arrives with a Skeleton Key

The inside
      and outside
            of the parts.

      Of needing.
Of want.

In seeing and believing
      the losing &
            choosing.

      Estranging

and changing
for meeting and greeting—

      the subtexts
            the wares /
for wanting
      the piercing
            of naked masks,
      cooled &

      congealing,

      a sobering touch
            afloat,
      a hope

      unspecified

Escape, come quickly

Space breaks
      & lifting you, is
            lifting me,
lifting us
      our endless
            search

as we bloom and sow

      between love's sorrows

Bats

Night surrenders,
its armistice aligned with temporary thresholds
        watching for what awaits the day

Bay Area Temporary Sanitation
        takes a hard turn, its houses teeter
                with salvage beleaguered,

a reminder that this shit can't possibly last forever

storefronts leak their shimmery shadows
        extending lashes to meet the light

the constancy of windows
        repackaged and retold,
        impermanence masked in dust & coolness,
                the secrecy of once having been sand

And there are those who find themselves
        only when all the world goes missing,
                sleepwalking
to do whatever can be undone

                as the length of hours gets recounted
        computed in the sadness of sidewalks
                & matters that burn all harbingers

        steps mediate the songs that
                grow through the cracks of plastic
        and fabricated fuckery

where earthly waters trickle
slapping our gills to leave behind

what is left

when windows close

our lungs uplifted

so that we are free to fly

& dream again

How time flies

what if we stopped wondering
what if we stopped asking: why
what if the ordinary became   extraordinary
what if things were— what if things   were
what if the scarcity dance

                 stopped dancing

                   and water pooled

                 in the palms

                   of our hands

what if. traces of faces. masks. that sing. a song with a veil in its heart.
because we're real and not really. because we are. a facade. a voice of a
face we wouldn't recognize. *otherwise.*

we don't know, yet we know so well. intimate at times. both tender and
kind. this inhabitance. the voice of a face has not one voice. each face
isn't. what we seem. because *sometimes* a face is not its voice.

because *sometimes* we don't hear. because *sometimes* we don't. how often
do we not. listen. that we follow faces whose voices are not. *sometimes* we
can't see our own face. we know watery skies can lure the most languid
of lovers.

gills and lungs, the sun sinks through skin, alive and breathing. many are
the watershed moments. because of the sparkly things. but stars in the
sky are not the issue.

& then the watershed said you are beautiful. all that you should be. and
so are we. all that you are, are we. beautiful as we hold. as we let on and
hold. to songs. music. symphonies. gatherings. impromptu. concerts.

jam sessions. orchestral bands. bloated throats drink wetland silk: their lesions sticky with lurid lessons. amphibious migration and the textures of love calls, nocturnal warriors drunk on the trill of desire. elastic chambers and sound pitched eyes. dragonflies muse through the night. bubbled sacs push panic buttons. sometimes it is the shrill to release me. when stress eases into silence. danger and love come close *sometimes*. maybe often. and i'm under your spell. the lovers, the dreamers, and i'm under your spell; the lovers, the

                                        dreamers

this must be magic. i know that this

                                    might just be

A Piscean Love Sonnet

Magnetic fields will guide you
        across this ocean floor

Silent scales will be renewed
        crescent moons endure

This pitted fruit aligns you,
        it winks across your skin

And welcomes not the seer
        that hides the shade within

In water world redemption
        you find yourself complete

Inverted caves unmentioned
        your fish eyes left to speak

This time is here and so we shift / to blue-laced shoal,
        our arms adrift.

ACKNOWLEDGMENTS

Endless gratitude and love for the exceptionally gifted Mills College professors and cohort (2023): Juliana Spahr, Truong Tran, Stephanie Young, Caroline, Em, Griffin, & Lyn. Thank you for your insight and guidance.

Word: Mother, Late to Work, and A Piscean Love Sonnet
    can be found in the author's chapbook, *Blends and Bends,* 2023
An excerpt of *dear bird* appeared in *Clever Fox* Issue 3, 2023
How Time Flies appeared in *The Ana,* Issue 13 2023
Nudity Arrives with a Skeleton Key appeared in
    Northridge Review, Spring 2022
Witness appeared in *The Raven's Perch,* 2022
Out and About appeared in *Troublemaker Firestarter,* Volume 2, 2022

DANA DEFRANCO is a writer and educator in the San Francisco Bay Area. Originally from New Jersey, Dana was born in Paterson and grew up in Passaic County. Her work explores the ways in which our humanity is both fragmented and healed within the everyday. Dana's poetry has been featured in many literary journals and magazines including *2RiverView, The Ana* and *BarBar*. Her chapbook, *Blends and Bends*, was published in June 2023 by Bottlecap Press. Dana holds an MFA in Creative Writing: Poetry from Mills College in Oakland. She is a full-time Pisces.

www.ingramcontent.com/pod-product-compliance
Lightning Source LLC
Chambersburg PA
CBHW030459130626
46549CB00007B/2782

9 781963 908473